# Seaside Treasures

## A Guidebook for Little Beachcombers

words & art by

*Sarah Grindler*

NIMBUS
PUBLISHING LTD.
— NIMBUS.CA —

Nimbus Publishing Limited
3660 Strawberry Hill Street, Halifax, NS, B3K 5A9
(902) 455-4286 nimbus.ca

Printed and bound in Canada

NB1416

Design: Heather Bryan
Editor: Penelope Jackson
Editor for the press: Emily MacKinnon

Library and Archives Canada Cataloguing in Publication

Title: Seaside treasures : a guidebook for little beachcombers / words and art by Sarah Grindler.
Names: Grindler, Sarah, author, illustrator.
Identifiers: Canadiana (print) 20189068264 | Canadiana (ebook) 20189068272 | ISBN 9781771087469 (hardcover) | ISBN 9781771087476 (HTML)
Subjects: LCSH: Beachcombing—Juvenile literature. | LCSH: Sea glass—Juvenile literature.
Classification: LCC G532 .G75 2019 | DDC j910.914/6—dc23

Nimbus Publishing acknowledges the financial support for its publishing activities from the Government of Canada, the Canada Council for the Arts, and from the Province of Nova Scotia. We are pleased to work in partnership with the Province of Nova Scotia to develop and promote our creative industries for the benefit of all Nova Scotians.

For my husband, Jason, and my extraordinary
family, who inspire me every day

A day of beachcombing is a day filled with salty sea air, enchanting seashells, and exciting discoveries.

The ocean holds so much beauty and adventure, and it leaves so many treasures on its shores. Let's explore these seaside treasures.

Have you ever gone beachcombing just after a storm, when the tide is out? Exciting pieces can get washed ashore, some that you would never expect.

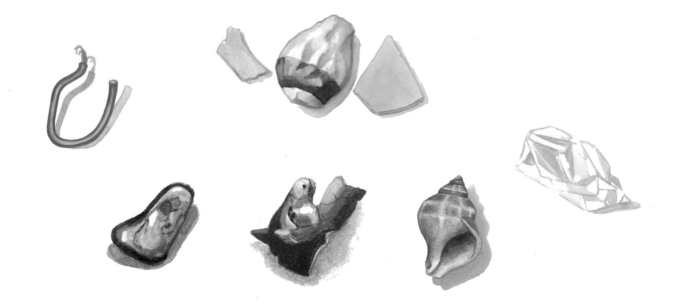

Some of my favourite treasures to find are purple sea urchin
shells. Urchins are round, spiky creatures that
sea otters love to munch on.

The beach is often covered with other colourful,
iridescent, and interesting shells like mussel shells,
sand dollars, and snail shells.

What do you think lived inside each of these
beautiful shells?

If you collect a shell, make sure there is no one home!

Another of my favourite treasures to find is blue sea glass.
Sea glass can be found in many colours, and some are rarer
than others.

Blue is not found as frequently as other colours,
and it could have come from old food jars or medicine
and drink bottles.

Have you ever found any?

Another rare colour of sea glass is purple.

Some pieces are from old purple bottles, but softer lavender
colours were actually once white or clear glass!
If the original glassmaker used a chemical called manganese,
the sun slowly turned the glass purple over time.

Isn't that amazing?

Other hard-to-find sea glass colours are red, orange, and yellow. You can find pieces of green, brown, and white glass more easily.

What is your favourite colour of sea glass?

These are glass fishing floats.

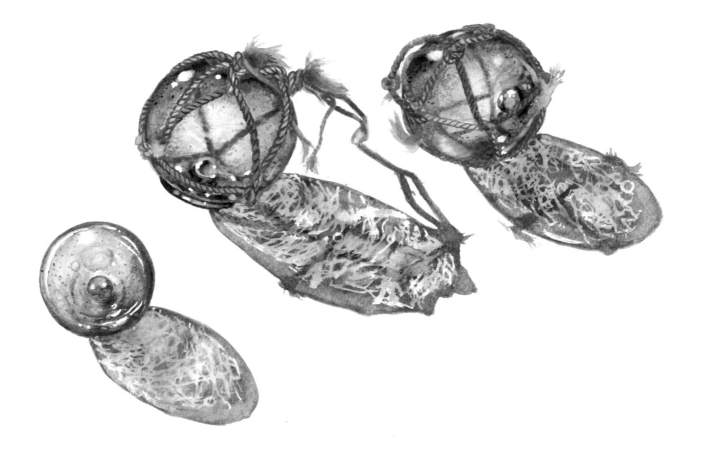

Fishers began using them almost two hundred years ago to keep their nets afloat. Some are the size of a tennis ball, while others are as big as a pumpkin!

Even though they are one of the least common treasures you can find, they still wash up on the beaches today. These three were found in Northern Japan.

What would you do if you found one?

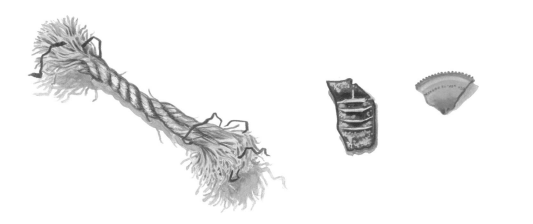

Around the Southern Gulf Islands of British Columbia,
you can find Coast Salish artifacts on the beaches. In Atlantic
Canada, there are sometimes Mi'kmaw, Maliseet, and
Beothuk artifacts hidden in the sand and rocks.

Indigenous people made all these tools long ago. What do
you think they used them for?

These are pieces of chinaware and silverware that
were lost in the sea.

What kind of dish do you think each piece is from?
I think I spy a teapot.

Do you wonder who might have used them?
Perhaps sailors, merchants, or pirates!

Amongst all the treasure that washes up on the beach, you can often find garbage. When I find garbage, I collect it to help keep our oceans and beaches clean.

Can you spot the garbage on these pages?

Treasure hunting at the seaside is such a joy,
and it's always full of surprises.

Now that you know about sea glass, chinaware, shells, and garbage, let's go back and look again at all the pictures in this book. Can you tell which is which?

Do you see any sea urchins? Can you guess what other treasures may have once been?

Just imagine what you can make with all
your seaside treasures!

And then, when you are finished, you can return
to the beach and hunt again.

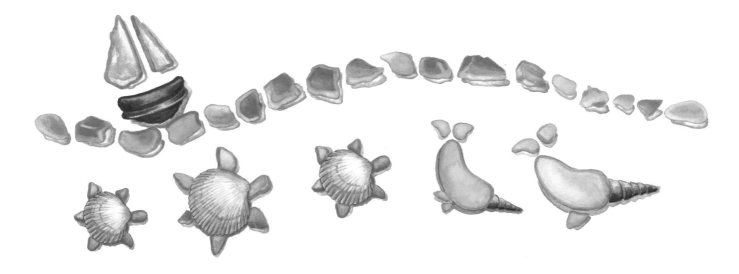

What will you find?